It was Rosie's birthday.

Grandad gave her a present.

Thank you

It was a spider.

Mum and Dad
gave her a present.

It was a kite.

Sam gave her a present.

It was a spaceship.

Mo gave her a present.

It was a book about monsters.

The postman gave
Rosie a big box.

to Rosie
love from
Aunty
Grace

Rosie opened the box.

Then Rosie gave everybody . . .

JULIE PARK
Monsters
MONSTERS
J. PARK

a terrible fright!